Drumming

Anne Teresa De Keersmaeker / Rosas
Steve Reich / Dries Van Noten / Jan Versweyveld

Photography
Herman Sorgeloos
Anne Van Aerschot

Texts
Noé Soulier
Gilles Amalvi
Tessa Hall and Julia Rubies Subiros

Mercatorfonds

Distributed outside Benelux by Yale University Press, New Haven and London

Cover photo
Herman Sorgeloos

Drumming

Noé Soulier

At first glance, *Drumming*'s most striking feature is its economy of means. The choreography that unfolds over an eponymous score by Steve Reich is derived entirely from a single movement phrase. But while Reich's score relies on a reduced number of compositional principles, Anne Teresa De Keersmaeker mobilizes for her piece highly heterogeneous compositional approaches. Behind the seeming homogeneity there is a true syncretism that appeals to models belonging to a multiplicity of mediums and eras. The use of geometry to determine the movements and relations between the dancers extends and renews a choreographic legacy that dates back to the *belle danse* of the seventeenth century. The thematic development and the general structure of the piece, for their part, show profound affinities with the sonata as it crystallized during the First Viennese School, around 1800. De Keersmaeker uses one proportion scale, the Fibonacci sequence, to structure different aspects of the composition—notably the space the dancers use, the duration of each section, and the number of dancers present in them—and this deployment of a single organizing principle to determine various parameters is for its part reminiscent of the serialism of the Second Viennese School, developed by Arnold Schoenberg, Alban Berg, and Anton Webern in the early twentieth century. Lastly, certain transformations in the movement phrase create a direct link with Reich's musical composition and, more generally, with the compositional perspectives that audiovisual recording technologies have opened up. This essay will analyze each of these layers in the composition of *Drumming* and observe how they unite in a coherent approach to the organization of space and time.

Experience and Recording

Drumming's choreography is constructed upon a movement phrase out of which De Keersmaeker derives two main transformations: retrograde and slow motion. These two transformations are directly connected to the experience of movement that has been made possible by film and video. The retrograde in *Drumming* consists of inverting not the order of movements, but rather the very flow of movement itself. It corresponds to the experience of rewinding a film and seeing the movements unfold in reverse, and thus is quite different from the way retrograde is used in serial music, where the reversal of the order of the notes does not modify them as sound events. It is a continuous retrograde, and not the inversion of discrete elements.

The technical possibility of recording and manipulating movement is what renders such an operation imaginable in the first place. There is a parallel here with certain compositional tools that Reich used, which are inseparable from the possibilities opened up by sound recording technology. The musical piece *Drumming* marks the culmination of one of the most emblematic of those possibilities, as Reich noted: "In the context of my own music, *Drumming* is the final expansion and refinement of the phasing process."[1] He discovered phasing while working with tape recordings for the creation of *It's Gonna Rain* (1965):

> I discovered the phasing process by accident. I had two identical loops of Brother Walter saying "It's gonna rain," and I was playing with two inexpensive tape recorders—one jack of my stereo headphones plugged into machine A, the other into machine B. I had intended to make a specific relationship: "It's gonna" on one loop against "rain" on the other. Instead, the two machines happened to be lined up in unison and one of them gradually started to get ahead of the other.[2]

This audio experience, made possible via the intermediary of the machine, turned out to be extremely rich musically: "As I listened to this gradual phase shifting process, I began to realize that it was an extraordinary form of musical structure. This process struck me as a way of going through a number of relationships between two identities without ever having any transitions. It was a seamless, uninterrupted musical process."[3]

Reich initially explored the musical potential of phasing in pieces composed for the tape recorder: *It's Gonna Rain* (1965) and *Come Out* and *Melodica* (both 1966). But it was with *Piano Phase*, in 1967, that he first realized it was possible for a human to perform the phasing process starting from a recording:

> Unfortunately, it seemed to me at the time impossible for two human beings to perform that gradual phase shifting process, since the process was discovered with, and was indigenous to, machines. On the other hand, I could think of nothing else to do with live musicians that would be as interesting as the phasing process. Finally, late in 1966, I recorded a short repeating melodic pattern played on the piano, made a tape loop of that pattern, and then tried to play against the loop myself, exactly as if I were a second tape recorder. I found, to my surprise, that while I lacked the perfection of the machine, I could give a fair approximation of it.[4]

Eventually, he did manage to perform the process with another musician and without a "mechanical aid":

> In the next few months, Arthur Murphy, a musician friend, and I, both working in our homes, experimented with the performance of this phase shifting process using piano and tape loops. Early in 1967, we finally had the opportunity to play together on two pianos and found, to our delight, that we could perform this process without mechanical aid of any kind.[5]

Thus, what had originally been a sound effect obtained thanks to the technological mediation of a tape recorder became a compositional principle:

> Looking back on the tape pieces that preceded *Piano Phase*, I see that they were, on the one hand, realizations of an idea that was indigenous to machines, and, on the other hand, the gateway to some instrumental music that I would never have come to by listening to any other Western, or for that matter non-Western, music.[6]

Working from a recording made it possible to enrich the sound experience, not only by revealing the possibility of an idea "indigenous to machines," but also by opening the door to an entirely new approach

1 Steve Reich, "Drumming," in *Writings on Music: 1965–2000*, ed. Paul Hilier (Oxford: Oxford University Press, 2002), 64.

2 Steve Reich, "It's Gonna Rain," in *Writings on Music*, 20–21.

3 Reich, "It's Gonna Rain," 20.

4 Steve Reich, "Piano Phase," in *Writings on Music*, 22.

5 Reich, "Piano Phase," 24.

6 Reich, "Piano Phase," 24.

to synchronization and the process of musical evolution. In *Fase, Four Movements to the Music of Steve Reich* (1982), De Keersmaeker makes the phasing process the principle of the choreography. The choreography, rather than being inspired by the video recording of movement, in fact constitutes a transposition to the medium of dance of a musical principle Reich discovered via the overlaying of audio recordings. In effect, two audio tracks can be present in the same sound space (as two musicians can be), but two video recordings cannot share the same visual space like two dancers can. If we use transparency to superimpose two videos, the dancers cannot cross each other, they cannot be in front of or behind one another. When they are in the same spot, they merge rather than mutually exclude one another, as two real bodies would do. However, the choreographic retrograde is inspired by one of the most immediate manipulations of video recordings: the fact that one can observe footage being played backward. In that respect, the retrograde is a less direct equivalent of the phasing process than that present in the choreography of *Fase*, though, in another respect, it is closer to what inspired its use—that is, the artistic exploration of an idea "indigenous to machines."

Recording tools—whether for fixed images, sound, or moving images—extend and transform our perceptive experience. The way Reich and De Keersmaeker use them to propose new operations has its roots in older artistic traditions. For instance, since its advent in the nineteenth century, photography has profoundly affected the history of painting. The works in Gustave Le Gray's series *Marines* (1856–57) that are photographs of waves had a decisive impact on landscape painting because they immobilized a previously elusive visual phenomenon. This influence is particularly manifest in Gustave Courbet's *La Vague* (The Wave, 1869). Edgar Degas was a photographer himself, and the pictures he took became an integral part of his creative process because they allowed models to explore new postures, not having to hold the same pose for as long, and painters radically renewed the nude.[7] This dialogue between painting and photography is still ongoing today, and we see it in the work of artists like Gerhard Richter and Luc Tuymans. In an interview with David Sylvester, Francis Bacon discussed how photography extended the realm of the sensible:

> I think one's sense of appearance is assaulted all the time by photography and by the film. So that, when one looks at something, one's not only looking at it directly but one's also looking at it through the assault that has already been made on one by photography and film. . . . Through the photographic image I find myself beginning to wander into the image and unlock what I think of as its reality more than I can by looking at it. And photographs are not only points of reference; they're often triggers of ideas.[8]

Recording technologies transform our relation to the visible and to sound by making it possible to fix and manipulate an ephemeral event so as to forefront a variety of dimensions that would have remained imperceptible in the absence of those technologies. In that, they do more than modify our experience of the particular event that has been recorded: they change the way we pay attention to experience. The fact that we can observe a movement that has been slowed down, or played in reverse motion, makes us aware of certain transitions that we had, until that moment, failed to detect. They transform what we can see in movement itself. So if photography allowed painting to represent fleeting events that had until then eluded it, and sound recordings enabled us to imagine new modes of synchronization, how has video recording transformed the perception of movement in dance? And more specifically in De Keersmaeker's case, what impact does the retrograde have on the experience of movement?

It is relatively easy to accomplish the retrograde transformation of a movement whose unfolding is controlled by muscular strength. For example, if someone moves her hand from left to right at a constant speed, the transformation can be achieved simply by moving it, at the same speed, from right to left. But if the movement also entails the action of one of the two exogenous forces that impact the body

—gravity and inertia—without them being constantly under the control of the muscular force, then reversing the movement becomes extremely difficult. For example, if someone drops her arm, or throws it up and allows the inertia of this momentum to define the trajectory of the movement—in other words, when a person momentarily abandons her body to the exogenous forces that act on it—it is impossible to really reverse the dynamic. That said, the very effort exerted in order to attempt this impossible transformation enables us to perceive the forces that act on the body, as well as the physical, mechanical dimension of the movement.

Retrograde is part and parcel of an approach to movement that first emerged at the end of the 1960s, notably in the work of choreographers like Trisha Brown and Simone Forti. Merce Cunningham was their immediate predecessor, and his vocabulary defined movement geometrically. His dancers strive to perform specific forms and trajectories with different parts of their bodies, whereas in Brown's work, movements are primarily approached as the result of forces that act on the body. Albeit in a different style, the same is at the center of De Keersmaeker's vocabulary in *Drumming*. We can interpret retrograde in Brown's work as a tool with which to underline a physical and mechanical approach to movement. The effort to invert the temporal direction of movement brings to the fore forces that are too familiar to be noticeable when movement follows its usual flow. There is an element of illusionism to the retrograde, since the effort is directed at reproducing a dynamic that, strictly speaking, cannot exist: the reversal of a fall, or of an élan. But the goal of the illusion is to render visible a fundamental dimension of the body and of movement: the body as a physical thing that belongs to the physical world and is subject to the same laws that govern the objects surrounding it.

Extended Geometry

In *Drumming*, the performance space is structured around an extremely precise geometry: "The basic structure of the spiral trajectory inscribed in the rectangle, dividing it into eight squares in growing size, is multiplied in order to provide every dancer with his or her own 'house.' The model is mirrored according to straight and diagonal axes so that it creates symmetrical spirals stage left and stage right, upstage and down-stage."[9] This organization of the dancers' trajectory follows an orthogonal geometry and a double symmetry that traces back to the very beginnings of choreography in the West. It is an organization that appears with particular clarity and sophistication in early eighteenth-century scores by Raoul Auger Feuillet. In these, the trajectory of each dancer, represented in a bird's-eye view, draws complex patterns that weave their way into the trajectories of the other dancers to form symmetrical figures. *Drumming* situates itself in this tradition while also breaking free, at least in part, from the orthogonal constraint:

> In addition to eight spirals, [Thierry] De Mey suggested shifting this rectangular construction, rotating it from its own center at a certain angle. This generated four more spirals, twelve in total, where each dancer could have his or her separate trajectory.[10]

Ballet, as it was then codified over the course of the nineteenth century, systematized the spatial organization of movement that it had inherited from the *belle danse* tradition of the seventeenth and eighteenth centuries. It relies on an orthogonal geometry to define the trajectory of the dancers as well as the forms and orientations of different parts of the body. Ballet has eight possible orientations, separated by 45-degree angles. It is very difficult to orient oneself in relation to angles tighter than that without some sort of visual anchor. In *Drumming*, De Keersmaeker managed to overcome this constraint by using markings on the floor: during rehearsals, these markings materialize the exact position of the squares that compose the "four more spirals." The angle that differentiates them is narrower than 45 degrees, but once the dancers have assimilated this spatial

7 For an in-depth study of the relations between painting and photography see Dominique de Font-Réaulx, *Painting and Photography: 1839-1914* (Paris: Flammarion; London: Thames and Hudson, 2012).

8 David Sylvester, *The Brutality of Fact: Interviews with Francis Bacon* (London: Thames and Hudson, 2016), 37.

9 Anne Teresa De Keersmaeker and Bojana Cvejić, *Drumming and Rain: A Choreographer's Score* (Brussels: Mercatorfonds and Rosas, 2014), 25.

10 De Keersmaeker and Cvejić, *Drumming and Rain*, 26. Thierry De Mey has been a frequent collaborator of Anne Teresa De Keersmaeker.

orientation during rehearsals, the floor markings can be removed without compromising the precision of the directions. The dancers using the "pivoted" rectangle as a spatial reference explore an interstice of the orthogonal organization inherited from ballet and thus break the omnipresence of that alignment.

This deviation is strengthened by the fact that the basic phrase is itself constructed on the series of squares that forms each spiral: "The phrase is composed in straight lines that point toward and touch the sides of the squares first, before they retrace the square in curved lines."[11] The body parts of one group form untold numbers of right angles and parallel lines, all of them arranged with relation to the same spatial referent, which corresponds to the architecture of the stage. The "pivoted" group, for its part, relies on an orthogonal framework whose coordinates are differently aligned. Because these two spatial frameworks are overlaid, they create friction in the geometric arrangement of the dancers. The choreography is constructed upon an orthogonal geometry that allows for enormous precision in the alignment between the dancers. But, by overlaying two different orthogonal frameworks, the choreography breaks the orthogonal coherence of the ensemble. In this way, *Drumming* simultaneously affirms and disturbs the orthogonal and symmetrical geometry inherited from ballet. It pushes the complexity and sophistication of that geometry to the extreme—to the point of breaking the orthogonal arrangement that usually guarantees its coherence.

Succession and Simultaneity

The use of retrograde belongs to a modern artistic tradition that questions the ways in which technical evolutions disrupt our relation to the world, while the approach through geometry is a continuation of a way of organizing space that has been part of dance ever since it first entered the theater in the West. The overall organization of De Keersmaeker's *Drumming* is part and parcel of a search for coherence between multiple parameters, in many ways akin to that explored by serial music. The piece uses the Fibonacci sequence—in which each number is the sum of the two previous ones: 1, 1, 2, 3, 5, 8, and so on—to determine many different aspects of the composition, for instance the scenic space: "The basic phrase traces a trajectory of a spiral unfolding in eight squares whose sizes result from dividing one rectangle into golden section proportions. This means that each square has different dimensions according to the Fibonacci sequence of progression."[12]

The Fibonacci sequence likewise governs the succession of the number of dancers in the exposition of the basic phrase: "*Drumming* starts with the exposition of the phrase in two phases: first, in a buildup from one dancer to two, to three, to five, to eight, and finally including everyone, and second, in a reverse process of reduction from twelve dancers to one dancer, always keeping the same combinations of dancers. In the Fibonacci sequence of progression, dancers gradually replace each other."[13] The sequence also determines the duration of each part or the exposition of the basic phrase:

> This effectively means that the time is spiraled as well. The longest will be [Cynthia] Loemij's exposition in the beginning, comprising eight units. With each new group, the number of units diminishes: while Loemij dances eight units, she and [Roberto] Oliván will dance five units, then the material will shrink into three units, and so on. The gradual reduction of the material follows the Fibonacci sequence as well. The more people, the less time and the quicker they have to abort the phrase.[14]

Time is treated spatially—it is "spiraled"—and space, for its part, is treated temporally. Or, better said, both depend on the same series of relations, namely the Fibonacci sequence. The fact that the simultaneity of events in space and their succession in time are regulated by the same principle reveals a proximity with Arnold Schoenberg's

twelve-tone compositions and the Second Viennese School. Indeed, with Schoenberg, the use of a series and its derivatives (transpositions, inversions, and retrogrades) to determine all the musical events made it possible to move past the traditional opposition between harmony and melody. According to Schoenberg, "The elements of a musical idea are partly incorporated in the horizontal plane as successive sounds, and partly in the vertical plane as simultaneous sounds. The mutual relation of tones regulates the succession of intervals as well as their association into harmonies."[15] The superposition and the succession of notes are governed by the same intervals so as to unify the different dimensions of the musical proposition: "*The two-or-more-dimensional space in which musical ideas are presented is a unit.*"[16]

Like Schoenberg, De Keersmaeker constructs her choreography using a single phrase, from which she generates several derivatives: the retrograde, the mirror, and the spatial transposition. Even if we should be careful not to force the comparison—the basic phrase does not play the same role in De Keersmaeker's piece as in a twelve-tone composition—there is the same ambition in *Drumming* to construct a coherent structure based on principles that apply to all the compositional parameters. If the series allowed Schoenberg to unify harmony and melody, the Fibonacci sequence allows De Keersmaeker to unify the organization of space and time.

Drumming opens with the exposition of the phrase first in retrograde, and then in its standard form. This phrase is subdivided into eight sections, which in their turn correspond to the eight squares that form each dancer's spiral, from the smallest to the largest. In its standard form, the space covered by the dancers in each part of the phrase is more and more stretched out. The number of dancers and the space covered in each section of the phrase increases, but the time devoted to each part decreases. These increases and decreases follow the first numbers of the Fibonacci sequence, from one to eight for the number of dancers, and from eight to one for the duration. This double movement creates an exponential densification of the choreographic events on stage: more and more dancers cover more and more of the scenic space in a tighter and tighter time frame. The spectators, however, likely cannot establish a direct connection between the impression of unity generated by this construction and the spatiotemporal relations just described. The structure is not only too complex and unfolds too rapidly, but certain elements are too cryptic to be directly identified. Yet they *experience* the proportional relations even if they are not directly aware of them.

This harmony—whose principles, once again, are not directly perceptible—differs greatly from Reich's compositional thinking in *Drumming*: "I am interested in perceptible processes. I want to be able to hear the process happening throughout the sounding music." He goes on to elaborate:

> What I am interested in is a compositional process and a sounding music that are one and the same thing. James Tenney said in conversation, "Then the composer isn't privy to anything." I don't know any secrets of structure that you can't hear. We all listen to the process together since it's quite audible, and one of the reasons it's quite audible is because it's happening extremely gradually. The use of hidden structural devices in music never appealed to me. Even when all the cards are on the table and everyone hears what is gradually happening in a musical process, there are still enough mysteries to satisfy all.[17]

Each of the processes present in *Drumming*, the musical piece, is clearly identifiable and listeners can hear their gradual unfolding. Reich pits this readability and transparency in hearing against the compositional principles of other musical movements:

> John Cage has used processes and has certainly accepted their results, but the processes he used were compositional ones that could not be heard when the piece was performed. The process

11 De Keersmaeker and Cvejić, *Drumming and Rain*, 21.
12 De Keersmaeker and Cvejić, *Drumming and Rain*, 20.
13 De Keersmaeker and Cvejić, *Drumming and Rain*, 30.
14 De Keersmaeker and Cvejić, *Drumming and Rain*, 34.
15 Arnold Schoenberg, "Composition with Twelve Tones," in *Style and Idea* (New York: Philosophical Library, 1950), 109.
16 Schoenberg, "Composition with Twelve Tones," 109.
17 Steve Reich, "Music as a Gradual Process," in *Writings on Music*, 34–35.

of using the *I Ching* or imperfections in a sheet of paper to determine musical parameters can't be heard when listening to music composed that way. Similarly, in serial music, the series itself is seldom audible. (This is a basic difference between serial—basically European—music, and serial—basically American—art, where the perceived series is usually the focal point of the work.)[18]

The retrograde, the phasing process, and the slow-motion version of the phrase are all clearly visible in De Keersmaeker's choreography, thus creating a direct link to Reich's score. But other aspects of the composition act in more subterranean ways, and belong more to the "European" than to the "American" approach (to borrow Reich's schematic distinction). That is the case, notably, with the use of the Fibonacci sequence as the common denominator with which to determine a host of different parameters: "The choreography divides into four sections, approximately following the musical macrostructure—'skin,' 'wood,' 'metal,' and finale. The 'wood' section is longer in choreography than in music, because it comprises the golden section in its end, which isn't in the middle, but rather closer to the second third of the piece."[19]

With the use of the golden section, which is directly derived from the Fibonacci sequence, we once again find the application of the same relational scale at the level of the piece as a whole. More importantly, however, the four-part structure of the choreography is very close to the classical structure of the sonata, itself emblematic of the "European" tradition. De Keersmaeker describes the two first parts as follows:

> The first part equals the exposition of the phrase unisono, in both senses—"going" and retrograde. What follows next is a simpler case of counterpoint on the basis of the same material—"same against the same"—where dancers execute the same material with time delays, that is, in canon. . . . The second part is constructed in extensive and rich counterpoint, where different cells are superimposed: for instance, cell 1 to cell 2, or cell 2 to cell 3, or even cell 3 to cell 6.[20]

The two opening parts correspond to the first movement of a sonata: the exposition of the first theme (here, the retrograde) and of the second theme (the phrase in "going"), and their development, whose complexity increases. This development, which relies on canons and fugue motifs, can be compared to the developments of the final five piano sonatas by Ludwig van Beethoven, from Opus 101 to Opus 111. The famous sonata number 29 in B major (Opus 106), known as the *Hammerklavier*, contains a fugal development of the first theme of the first movement, and a fugue inserted into the final movement. In his late works, Beethoven accomplished a synthesis between two canonical forms of instrumental music, the fugue and the sonata, by incorporating the contrapuntal science of the former into the structure of the latter. De Keersmaeker integrates this synthesis in the overall structure of *Drumming*. The third part corresponds to the slow movement of a sonata: "I will call it the 'slow phrase.' In contrast to the previous part, as well as to the music it is danced to, it begins in a slow tempo."[21] And the last part also corresponds to the structure of a sonata:

> The fourth part, or the finale, recapitulates and superimposes all the choreographic devices used until then: complex shifts in space with both straight and curved lines, phase shifting, counterpoint using different materials, acceleration and deceleration, and so on. This part includes an incomplete retrograde recapitulation of several sections, such as, most strikingly, the exposition from the beginning.[22]

The contrasts in tempo and intensity; the expositions, re-expositions, and developments in the first, second, and fourth parts; and the overall architecture of the piece are all clearly inherited from the canonical form of the sonata as it was defined in Western music with the First Viennese School, but whose origins Schoenberg traced all the way back to Johann Sebastian Bach: "He was also the first to introduce just that technique so necessary for the progress of their New Music: the technique of 'developing variation,' which made possible the style of the great Viennese Classicists."[23] This underlying structure gives a sense of coherence to the unfolding of an abstract proposition over a long time frame. This coherence does not rely on the direct identification of the mechanisms of its construction; it is instead grasped intuitively, thanks to our familiarity with a structure that has sedimented over time.

In her overall conception of composition, De Keersmaeker clearly belongs to the "European" approach, to return to Reich's distinction, whose major representatives in the first half of the twentieth century were Schoenberg and his twelve-tone composition. The shared treatment of time and space, together with the use of the contrapuntal development characteristic of the structure of the sonata, show that, with *Drumming*, De Keersmaeker aligns herself with a compositional approach that is rooted in the European tradition of classical music, from the polyphony of Renaissance masters to the post-serialism of the years following World War II. This anchoring creates a stark contrast with Reich's ambition, during the 1960s and 1970s, to break with that tradition by thinking composition itself as a gradual, and fully perceptible, process—a break that entailed abandoning most of the compositional tools bequeathed by the First and Second Viennese Schools.

Compositional Syncretism

In *Drumming*, De Keersmaeker gathers extremely heterogeneous approaches to composition into a coherent whole in which each undergoes a profound transformation. What is at stake is not an eclecticism in which sometimes contradictory approaches are simply juxtaposed, but a syncretism in which their sense is transformed by the new roles they have been given. For instance, the "slow phrase" can be read as a modification of the original phrase inspired by video recording. It transforms the perception of movement, the way slow motion does in a film, but it also occupies the traditional position of the slow movement in a sonata. Moreover, De Keersmaeker does not apply the slowing down of movement uniformly to the entire sequence; instead, she punctuates the sequence with abrupt accelerations that are reminiscent of the dotted rhythms and strong rhythmic contrasts of Beethoven's slow movements. In so doing, the "slow phrase" creates a synthesis between a classical music form and the change that fairly recent recording technologies have brought about in how movement is perceived.

At first sight, the use of the phasing process, borrowed from Reich, in the thematic development of the piece might seem to be a contradiction in terms, given that Reich used it to break with the logic of "development by variation" inherited from European music thanks to a perfectly gradual process of transformation. In *Drumming*, the compositional tool that was meant to evade thematic development is paradoxically made to serve precisely that kind of development. That way of using it underlines another dimension of the phasing process, namely the richness of its contrapuntal possibilities. Reich himself analyzed phasing as a new canon form:

> In retrospect, I understand the process of gradually shifting phase relationships between two or more identical repeating patterns as an extension of the idea of infinite canon or round. Two or more identical melodies are played with one starting after the other, as in traditional rounds, but in the phase shifting process the melodies are usually much shorter repeating patterns, and the time interval between one melodic pattern and its imitation(s), instead of being fixed, is variable. Nevertheless, that this new process bears a close family resemblance to the thirteenth century idea of round seems to give it some depth. Good new ideas generally turn out to be old.[24]

18 Reich, "Music as a Gradual Process," 35.
19 De Keersmaeker and Cvejić, *Drumming and Rain*, 27–28.
20 De Keersmaeker and Cvejić, *Drumming and Rain*, 28.
21 De Keersmaeker and Cvejić, *Drumming and Rain*, 28.
22 De Keersmaeker and Cvejić, *Drumming and Rain*, 28.
23 Arnold Schoenberg, "New Music, Outmoded Music, Style and Idea," in *Style and Idea*, 43.
24 Reich, "It's Gonna Rain," 20.

It is precisely as "an extension of the idea of infinite canon" that De Keersmaeker mobilizes the phasing process in *Drumming* alongside other, more traditional forms of canon. Phasing, that idea "indigenous to machines," thus touches hands with the perpetual canon, one of the oldest forms of musical polyphony.

In *Drumming*, De Keersmaeker operates a fusion between three different traditions: the spatial organization inherited from ballet; compositional tools inherited from the European musical tradition; and an exploration of how the technological evolutions characteristic of modernity have transformed our perception. By extending them to geometric space, she succeeds in giving a new dimension to the compositional tools inherited from serialism. She likewise brings to the fore the profound links binding processes inspired by technical evolution to old compositional forms. This fusion gives new meaning not just to the classical forms themselves, but also to the mutations of sensible experience linked to technological mutations. It may be that the common point between an ancient compositional form, like the perpetual canon, and the recording technology that made the phase shifting process possible, or between the experience of slow motion in a video and an adagio in a sonata, is the fact that they are tools that allow us to modulate and organize our experience. Our way of perceiving our surroundings is at least in part fashioned, whether consciously or unconsciously, by the compositional forms we have inherited. They structure how we develop, and how we interpret, the new ways of recording the world that technological evolutions are continuously making available to us. These, in their turn, shed new light on canonical forms. Where one might see only an opposition between tradition and modernity, *Drumming* shows us the profound links that run through the many and varied tools with which we give form to experience.

Interview with Anne Teresa De Keersmaeker by Gilles Amalvi

Gilles Amalvi — In 1998, you returned to the composer Steve Reich with *Drumming*, a production that marked a new phase in your oeuvre. Reich's music had allowed you to invent your vocabulary in 1982, with *Fase*. What prompted this return to Reich almost twenty years later?

Anne Teresa De Keersmaeker — I conceived *Fase*, and more specifically the solo *Violin Phase*, when I was living in New York in 1981. At that time, I knew two compositions by Reich: *Violin Phase*, from 1967, and *Drumming*, from the early 1970s. I can recall as if it were today the Deutsche Grammophon triple album of *Drumming*, with yellow-tipped mallets on the cover. I think *Drumming*—or maybe it was Philip Glass's *Einstein on the Beach*—was my first encounter with minimalist music. As a self-taught choreographer, I advanced in stages. *Violin Phase* is a fifteen-minute solo; it was still very simple, very compressed. I thought *Drumming* was a fascinating composition, but I also saw it as something beyond my reach at that time.

While I was at work on *Violin Phase*, I listened often to Johann Sebastian Bach's fifth Brandenburg Concerto. There was something about those compositions, I mean *Drumming* and Bach's concerto, that was too much, too ambitious. They were too big, too complex, too long. In sum, they were way too much! They felt like insurmountable challenges, and it took me a long time before I felt ready to take them on. That's why I chose to work on Reich's earlier compositions—they just felt more in line with what I could do. That said, the desire to choreograph some of his longer and more complex pieces stayed with me, and so I decided to return to that desire in the late 1990s when I was looking for a musical composition that could become an entire program unto itself. I should also say, though, that I had already worked with *Drumming* in 1997, in a piece with my sister, Jolente, entitled *Just Before*.

Above and beyond this choreographic desire, it seems to me that *Drumming* is a key work of Reich's, a piece that marked a turning point for him. Indeed, it was the immediate predecessor of *Music for 18 Musicians*, which introduced harmony to his work. There is a programmatic dimension to *Drumming*. It's visible already in the title, where Reich introduces different kinds of percussion: on skin, wood, or metal. *Drumming* is the affirmation of a processual music. It is simultaneously a statement of minimalism and an exhilarating work that overflows with a sort of sovereign joy. That's what drew me to it, I think, much as with Bach, in a way: the absolute rigor of minimalism, the exhilarating power of rhythm, the simplicity of basic beats, and all the combinations that flow from that.

Reich went to West Africa to study polyrhythmic structures, and he also studied Balinese music. The polyrhythmic approach converged with his obsession for repetition and variations. He started to work with a ReVox, producing loops, inversions, and the like. His trajectory is essentially a path toward acoustic music, toward the materiality of instruments. *Drumming* combines the minimalist approach of his early works with a rhythmic dynamic that invites dance. Other influences on Reich include Bach, the Brandenburg Concertos in particular, but also the work of John Coltrane, and even some medieval music, like Pérotin. What all these influences have in common is a commitment to the idea of "maximizing the minimum." These are all different kinds of music, the fruit of very different sensibilities and thought processes, but Reich seems to have extracted from them a certain idea of music as a process; of abstraction rendered physical, embodied; of rhythm as a division of time. Maybe the best way to capture the idea is by referring to the title of a book by Fernand Schirren, who taught rhythm at the École Mudra in Brussels, and who was an important figure for an entire generation of Belgian choreographers: *Rhythm: Primordial and Sovereign*.

GA — As a choreographer, you have often choreographed musical compositions thought to be impossible to dance to—music by Arnold Schoenberg, John Coltrane, Gérard Grisey, and others. *Drumming*, on the other hand, is a "perfect" composition for dance: it allows for a wide variety of movements, which you are free to combine in myriad ways.

ATDK — The main challenge for me was to figure out how to write for a larger group of dancers over a longer period of time—more than an hour—and still manage to achieve something fluid, a sort of choreographic flow. That's what I did again with *Rain*, but *Drumming* was the first piece that really had this dimension for me. But I think there were other influences at play in the way I approached *Drumming*. For one, it's the piece I was working on when my dance school, P.A.R.T.S., was just getting started. Also, it coincided with the moment I started to discover Trisha Brown's work, particularly *Set and Reset*. The idea of working with very long phrases that unfold spirally following the proportions of the golden section—and not just the gestural cells, as in *Fase* or *Rosas danst Rosas*—comes in part from that discovery. It is true that the golden section and spirals were already present in my work, but in *Drumming* I wanted to use them to develop a piece for a large group, a piece whose temporal unity would be based entirely on a single musical score that could sustain the whole choreography. And that meant that I had to rethink their modalities.

I wrote a long phrase beginning with my own body as a starting point. That's how I used to start all my pieces, though eventually I withdrew in order to work more on the counterpoint composition. For *Drumming*, I had to go to the studio, alone, to construct that phrase, which served as the starting point for the choreography. From that phrase, we proceeded to deploy a minimalist syntax conceived as a mirror play: a mirror in space, by playing on the positions, and a mirror in time, by working the phrasing both forward and backward. The formal tools mobilized in the piece are extremely varied and form a truly abstract scale, so to speak. There is likewise a gap in time and space: for example we can start with a superimposition, in which two dancers perform the phrase in unison, and then gradually introduce a gap, so that the dancers are no longer in sync.

GA — *Drumming* is the "perfect" musical composition for a choreography, and the difficulty lies precisely in the fact that the match is almost too perfect. How did you manage to invent your own style, without sticking too closely to the structures specific to the music?

ATDK — Yes, that is the challenge when you work with a Steve Reich composition—it was already the case with *Fase*, in fact. Dance borrows from music, draws its inspiration from musical structures and their modes of articulation, which choreography uses to construct its own vocabulary and to produce an organization of movement in space and time. The idea of working with underlying geometric structures was already present in *Violin Phase*, and that idea is fundamental because it creates the possibility of organizing space and the stream of movements. A very important concept in *Drumming*, one that allowed me to work with a larger group in a smaller space, is the concept of the house. Each dancer has a "house," a portion of the space that belongs to him or her. The heart of the spiral is the house—the dancers can venture outside it and roam the space, but they must always start from a specific point in space, a defined anchoring point. And all the dancers know they can "go back home." That allows the phrase combinations not to become a huge chaos of disordered movements. And allows also, and simultaneously, for the creation of singularity, of effects of individuality, rather than an indeterminate mass of bodies and group movements.

GA — That's also what allows the gaze of the viewer to orient itself with respect to what it sees. Because audiences can follow the construction of the movement at the individual and the collective level, they can discern the complexity of the composition.

ATDK — Yes, and I think part of the reason for that is that *Drumming* bears the traces of the research that went into its making. As I mentioned, the first thing I did was to write the long phrase anchored to a spiral trajectory that served as my starting point. I then split that phrase into right and left, and then I wrote it backward, in retrograde. All the dancers had to learn the phrase so well that they could perform every permutation of it: in sync with other dancers and out of sync, in slow motion, forward and backward, et cetera. The choreography was constructed from that work in progress, if I may put it that way. The piece opens by showing the phrase backward, in retrograde. Then the phrase is doubled, in a construction based on the Fibonacci sequence. All the mathematical structures are used freely: we adapt them to the framework, to the dancers, and so on.

One of the principles we used to produce the passage of relays is the short backward and forward loops, which at Rosas we usually call "video-scratch." The procedure here involves taking a small piece of the phrase (we refer to it as a "cell"), looping it, and then dancing it both forward and backward (that is, in retrograde). Two dancers start doing it together, but gradually they fall out of sync—it's the principle at work in *Fase*. Once that was in place, we were able to start composing in space: a dancer starts the phrase on cell 1; another dancer, physically near, joins the phrase on cell 2, another on cell 3, and so on. For the most part, we didn't do much with the upper body because we wanted the focus to be on the displacements, on the inscription of patterns in space using various geometric figures: squares, curves, and pentagrams.

The phrase effects a movement of flux and reflux for the length of the piece, like a wave. Variations graft themselves onto it, accumulating and creating new patterns. And then there is the flux and reflux of the dancers: a single dancer, then two, then three, five, eight, until finally the entire group is on stage. In the middle are longer sequences composed of quartets, trios, duos, and so on. But the phrase is always present in one way or another, sometimes quite visibly and sometimes more discreetly. It's like a current, running underwater in some places and surfacing in others.

The last part is composed entirely of spatial motifs. Following the spiral structure, the dancers roam the whole stage very quickly, passing by or intersecting one another. At the end, the patterns of the phrase, which had until that moment been fixed, are transformed into a huge movement, with all the bodies turning in the space.

GA — There are moments in the piece when, instead of dancing, a dancer just walks around while very intense movements are going on around her. What sort of contrast did you want to create with that?

ATDK — It's always been my tendency to believe that any and every problem you encounter during the making of a piece can be turned into an advantage. To make it possible for all the dancers to find their "house," we had to work with walking. As it happens, not that long before the premiere, a few of the dancers got injured, probably because of the intense rehearsals. I thought about replacing them, but then it occurred to me that, since some of the developments of this phrase are very intense, why should there not be dancers who just walk? Why shouldn't some dancers dance the phrase, and others simply walk it? In other words, why not have dancers who follow the trajectory of the phrase, but on another frequency? I went on to develop that idea further—indeed, later on I even made it a basic principle of my work, to wit: *my walking is my dancing*. Walking is a starting point, a way of moving from one place to another, to organize one's body in space. It's also a displacement of one's center of gravity. I think *Drumming* is the first piece where that idea manifested itself clearly to me, and I really love watching this walking body give a secret beat to the piece while the other dancers are moving intensely to the lively rhythm.

The Dance That Keeps on Giving

Tessa Hall and Julia Rubies Subiros

Every three years, a new group of students enrolls at P.A.R.T.S., the dance school Anne Teresa De Keersmaeker founded in 1995. Among many other subjects in the curriculum, each group is required to learn a choreography from De Keersmaeker's repertoire. As early as their auditions, Generation 12 (2016—19) began work on *Drumming* (1998), and continued to do so for its three years at P.A.R.T.S., culminating in an adaptation of the ensemble piece for its graduation festival. In what follows, two students from Generation 12, Tessa Hall and Julia Rubies Subiros, speak about their unique experiences with the work, how it formed them as dancers and as people, and the ideas they brought to a piece that was created around the time they were born. Theirs is a reflection about what survives, and what changes.

The doors on each side of the room fly open and more than forty students, hailing from the four corners of the globe, enter in single file. One after the next, they line up along the sides of the space. Silence. The last students arrive and take their places at the end of each line. Everyone is ready. Rosas Performance Space, a big black-box theater adjoining the school, is vibrating in anticipation. The emptiness, the enveloping blackness, the waiting, the tension, the thrill. Drumming is about to begin.

Julia Rubies Subiros — It was in that same space that we learned this choreography for the first time, during our auditions for P.A.R.T.S. The first time the jury (which always includes Anne Teresa De Keersmaeker herself) saw us dance this piece, our individual performances determined whether we'd continue to the next phase of the audition process or be sent home.

Tessa Hall — Once we were accepted into P.A.R.T.S. and our classes began in December 2016, *Drumming* was the first piece from the Rosas repertoire that we encountered. The students were split into three groups, and each group had its teachers. Julia and I were in a group that started out with Marta Coronado and finished with Ursula Robb, both of whom had been original members of the cast when *Drumming* premiered in 1998. They transmitted to us what they had created twenty years earlier.

And our relationship with *Drumming* endured from our arrival all the way to the final second of our graduation festival. For some it will continue on.

J — Some students will go on to perform this work professionally. Others will write about it, and some will whip it out at parties.

T — Or at the beach in Oostende, in the back garden at P.A.R.T.S., in nightclubs, on the busy streets of Taipei, while warming up for any old class on any old day. It's the kind of dance that keeps on giving.

J — Some will remember it with tenderness, others won't want to touch it again, and still others will ask themselves, twenty years from now, whether they danced the phrase "right" or "left," and no doubt their muscle memory will take over at that point. This is how it goes, and how it continues.

T — Like any relationship, it has its ups and downs. There are moments of intimacy and profound connection, and moments of resistance and overkill; moments when you don't make sense together, but also moments when you learn a lot about yourself and one another; moments of growth and change, moments of pleasure and pure joy when you couldn't feel any better in your own skin, but also moments when you want to say goodbye forever because you've had enough. That's how it goes, and how it continues.

Drumming is about to begin. And here we are, waiting in the two lines, ready to go. Like horses about to race, the excitement ticking inside. It happens every time.

T — *Drumming* is the perfect piece to teach students, and over the years it has become one of the most popular pieces to use in workshops, for both aspiring dancers and amateurs. For a while now, Julia and I have been trying to figure out why this is so.

Anne Teresa built *Drumming* with one long base phrase based on the Fibonacci sequence, which is marked on the stage floor. The phrase starts off in a small "house" and grows in size until it spirals its way out of the biggest square on the Fibonacci floor. Its language is inspired by what it is danced upon: squares and spirals. It is at once a logical and an imaginative phrase because of the way it converses with the spaces of the squares (the corners and the straight edges), and because of the way the spirals weave their way across this geometric pattern.

Anne Teresa kneaded this cleverly designed base phrase into multiple forms through the use of simple choreographic tools, which she applied with expert craftsmanship. That said, the base phrase is what anyone dancing this piece, student or professional, must learn first, before any choreographic operations can be applied. It is the perfect choreography for young dancers in training not just because of the way it improves technique, but also because it imparts so much about what it means to dance with color, texture, tone, and suspension. Most important, it just feels good to dance it.

J — Like when the "Stars" section begins. It's one of my favorite parts. Fellow dancers Tessa, Némo, and I walk to one edge of the stage, form a triangular cluster, and look at each other before we take off. We breathe in, and we skip together while dashing through, out, and around various moving clusters, keeping the same foot pattern. We check in with each other; we all have huge smiles on; we rocket around the stage; we continue with the *chassés*. We feel like a team vivaciously moving together through an environment that is ever-changing and fluid. These and other moments feel ridiculously joyful, also thanks to the fact that we're dancing with friends. Who would have thought that a Fibonacci spiral overlaid with choreographic material could produce so much?

T — Once the base phrase has been learned, choreographic operations are added in/on/around/through/beneath/on top of it, eventually composing the phrase into the piece that is *Drumming*. For students, this makes *Drumming* a piece to learn about retrograde, canon, phase shifting, mirroring, altering one's front, slowing down and speeding up, poetic license or personal transformation, partnering, video scratching. These are all simple choreographic tools, but dancers must have them in their knowledge bank if they are to understand the compositional possibilities of dance, in the same sense that a painter in training learns about perspective, light and shade, various ways to use a brush, different types of paint, and so on.

J — The version of *Drumming* that we danced as students produced a dramaturgy that reflects very closely the operations used at each moment, from retrograde to the build-up section, to canon, to the phase-shifting block. From the inside, we could break the work down to whatever choreographic principle was in play at that time. In our hands, the work displayed its excellent craft and use of compositional techniques to the audience. At least, we were convinced that this is how the dramaturgy of the original worked. Then we saw the original a few months ago and realized that it's nothing like that!

T — Actually, Anne Teresa once discussed *Drumming* as a canvas.

J — When performed by the company, the original version is like an ocean, in that its structures are barely recognizable. It is easy to lose track of what's happening. Like a charged and vibrant aquarium, it invites another form of looking, more contemplative and wondrous.

T & J — There is something about how information travels between dancers—about the cues from one thing to the next, the elements that emerge and disappear, the calculated interferences, the crossings and relays—that is quite reminiscent of the movement of masses at train stations. *Drumming* has the same constant, pulsating busyness, the same clockworked chaos, but nothing is even a second late.

Whatever reason various people might have for being at a train station, they are all there for movement—the movement of the trains themselves, picking people up and dropping off, of jobs to be done and people to see. Some may be there to pick someone up and others to say goodbye. They are on their own trajectories, with different itineraries and destinations. Each person has a place to be, somewhere to get to, and no time to lose. Nothing stays still for long at a train station. Even those who *are* still, the people waiting, are not really still at all because they are likely in a state of anticipation. The trains pull in to the platforms but never stay too long, and some stay only for an urgently quick moment. Looking across the platforms, one perceives a certain polyrhythm. Moments link to moments—as one thing ends, another begins. The train will arrive at this particular minute; the people will be ready and waiting to jump on or off; a whistle indicates an imminent departure. Precision in the chaos.

J — We try to imagine what the times were like when Anne Teresa built that basic phrase, how her context seeped into it, how the realms of production influenced the work. We wonder what this piece would reflect if it had been made today, if it had been influenced by immaterial technologies, extreme globalization, the accelerationism of late capitalism.

Maybe Anne Teresa has already generated a response to these times in a different way. The generation we belonged to at P.A.R.T.S. participated in the Slow Walk in Paris in 2018, and again in Bruges in 2019: on both occasions, we walked in slow motion for four hours. The idea was to use slowness to create perspectives that contrast with the pace of daily life, and thereby leverage art as an instrument of critique.

T — On top of all that, to dance *Drumming* as a student is to learn perhaps the most important thing about dancing in an ensemble, which is, precisely, to learn what it is to be part of an ensemble. This is no doubt the hardest thing. Being in a relationship with *Drumming* for three-plus years alongside the other members of our group wasn't always easy or fun. We argued a lot, particularly about how to operate in unison, how to listen to one another, where to look, what the rhythm of this or that was, whose job it was to give the cue for one thing or another, who would be dancing in any particular section, who would be waiting on the sides, who had solos and duets, who didn't have any special roles, which corner of the square we should be in and when, who was drawing the focus. We had arguments over the fact that people forgot things, like when to come in (which happened to me a lot!), and so on and so forth.

It all comes down to figuring out how to exist in a community. How to achieve a balance between asserting one's individuality, needs, desires, and agency, and assuming one's responsibility in the functioning of the community. Considering one's contribution to the environment that we share with others. It's a peculiar line between freedom and responsibility. But then again, maybe freedom also lies in the responsibility that emerges when, as an individual, you take pride in your role within the wider picture. Perhaps *Drumming* is a metaphor for community—not only for the dancers performing it, but also for the audience, who sees in it something like a community in action.

Still in the line, shoulder to shoulder, waiting to start, we look to the right and to the left, peering into one another's eyes, making sure that our shoulders align. We all seem ready.

T — Speaking of community, I think that is exactly how it is to be a student at P.A.R.T.S. Maybe that's why, to make a comfortable generalization, P.A.R.T.S. students get so much out of their experience with *Drumming*, why they so easily relate to it each in their own way, shape, and form. It's a choreographic manifestation of their community at P.A.R.T.S., of what they are already in, developing through, learning to love, and coming into conflict with.

J — A few days before our final performance at the graduation ceremony, Anne Teresa read us a letter she wrote to dance. In it, she speaks of "the question of how to organize a multitude. Choreography is about writing the 'people.'" The letter continues:

> Choreography, like politics, is always a matter of agency, and how one might go about imagining a form of agency that is collective but not unconscious. People in a crowd waiting for a bus certainly share a sense of collectivity. But they do not necessarily share a sense of agency. In the same way, a crowd moving through a metro station on a busy morning might be said to exhibit traits of a "choreography"; given the architecture of the space, the crowd tends to move in a certain direction and generate specific patterns of movement.
>
> But people don't necessarily have any sense of the conscious moves they undertake within their environment. It is only when this group of people decides to go beyond this passive activity that one can truly speak of "dance." When "intention" and "agency" enter the picture, choreography as an art form makes its appearance. People treading through a train station on a Sunday morning are not necessarily dancing; people treading through a train station singing "Singing in the Rain" might be said to "dance" in a more convincing way.

T — Back in 2017, we performed *Drumming* in our three separate groups—the groups we had been working with for this piece since the beginning of our studies. In October 2018, we (the students of Generation 12) performed *Drumming* once again in this constellation at the Centre National de la Danse in Paris as part of a retrospective of Anne Teresa's work. On the way back to our hostel, three of us—Calvin Carrier, Jean-Baptiste Portier, and I—talked about *Drumming*, and about how we would like to experience it/work with it/perform it/relate to it from that point onward. We were in the midst of planning our graduation festival, and we knew that it would include *Drumming*. The question was *how* we would include it.

GXII Festival would take place over twelve days. From the beginning, we were unanimous about the fact that *Drumming* would be on the program, since it had played such a pivotal role in our development over our three years at P.A.R.T.S. The point of the *GXII Festival* was for everyone to present, or take part in, what they were proud of. The sense of pride functioned as the filter for what would and would not be included in the program, and *Drumming* was the piece that unified us the most. Basically, whatever relationship each individual had with *Drumming*, it was to some extent a positive one. *Drumming* made us feel empowered. It made us feel good and proud, and that was its unifying force.

Although we were sure it needed to be included, Calvin, Jean-Baptiste, and I were also certain that we didn't want to do it as it had always been done. Then it occurred to us that it was a pity that we had been split into the same three groups for so long: Would it not be amazing if we mixed the groups? Or even better, if we all danced the piece together? If the piece gave Generation 12 a sense of unity, then surely the best way to demonstrate this was to perform it all together.

That's when we came up with the idea of enlarging the scale of the piece. What if we took the entire floor of the Rosas Performance Space and laid three *Drumming* stages down on it, side by side? What if all three groups—all forty-four students of Generation 12—danced *Drumming* simultaneously, maybe even blended into one? It was going to be the ultimate, mega, celebratory *Drumming*.

But first: we had to ask Anne Teresa what she thought. It was her creation, and we needed her approval. We sketched out and approached her with what was still a fairly vague and premature proposal, full of holes and unanswered questions. Still, we had a vision built on enthusiasm and ambition. Anne Teresa said yes, and offered ideas on how to develop our concept. We were pretty excited. She trusted us with her work and put it in our hands, a gesture that was humbling, but also added fuel to our fire.

J — Anne Teresa has over the years treated *Drumming* differently from her other pieces. She has allowed it to be chewed on, changed, torn and reconstructed, no doubt because its strong foundations allow this. *Drumming* is one of the most malleable pieces in her repertoire: it serves the growth of the group performing it while still very much carrying out the choreographic dexterity that the work offers. Because of this, and due to its significance to our group, Anne Teresa was very happy to hear that we wanted to produce a unique version for the *GXII Festival*.

T — I'm sure she must have been a bit worried about what we would come up with, especially given the shortage of time. But, with the help of Rosas dancers Taka Shamoto, Clinton Stringer, Jakub Truszkowski, and Sandy Williams, we got there. It was an honor to play with the possibilities of *Drumming* in this manner, particularly after such a laborious and educational relationship with it. We considered ourselves extremely fortunate to be able to take the encounter with *Drumming* that many previous generations at P.A.R.T.S. have had—and that future students will continue to have—to another level. Since the *GXII Festival* was built on the idea that we would share what "we are proud of," it only seemed fitting to open and close the festival with *Drumming*.

We wait for the drum. All that is to happen is
laid out in front of us, just as it has innumer-
able times for many dancers before us. The immaterial dance vocabulary and architecture is in the
room, awaiting our last entrance as one group.
Pum . . . Pum . . . Pum. Ya!

T — Dancers in *Drumming* rely on a screen timer for cues. It occurred to us that when we reached our last performance of the festival, our last performance at P.A.R.T.S., this timer would be counting down the last seconds of this chapter in our lives. It's a funny thing to experience time so literally, so dramatically: there they go, the three final seconds of a three-year period. It was an exceedingly special moment.

J — When you dance this piece, you're dancing it not only with the people in the room alongside you, but also with people in the past who have done so, with every generation of P.A.R.T.S. that came before, and with the coming generations who will dance it in the future. The piece unfolds and circulates through so many bodies. It is a vocabulary, or lines of code, if you will, that many dancers have chewed on and digested, leaving behind a sediment that will continue to pulsate through new bodies in different ways.

T — When you see it, you think of community: of the community onstage whose members are the current guardians of the piece, people like Julia and myself, whose dance education was shaped by our relationship to it; of those who have taught it; of those who play its music; of those who produce and design it; of those who capture it on camera; of the imagined communities who will meet it in the future. And of you, the community attending a performance of *Drumming*— you are part of it, too.

J — We look forward to seeing how *Drumming* will continue to expand and generate new communities—to seeing how the material, touched and touching, can go to places still unimagined.

This is how it goes, and how it continues.

Drumming

Choreography
Anne Teresa De Keersmaeker

Created in 1998 with
Iris Bouche, Bruce Campbell, Marta Coronado, Alix Eynaudi, Fumiyo Ikeda, Martin Kilvády, Oliver Koch, Cynthia Loemij, Roberto Oliván de la Iglesia, Ursula Robb, Taka Shamoto, Rosalba Torres

Cast members between 1998 and 2016
Polina Akhmetzyanova, Boštjan Antončič, Linda Blomqvist, Beniamin Boar, Iris Bouche, Bruce Campbell, Marta Coronado, Stanislav Dobák, Tale Dolven, José Paulo dos Santos, Alix Eynaudi, Bryana Fritz, Jordi Galí, Carlos Garbin, Tarek Halaby, Fumiyo Ikeda, Anneleen Keppens, Martin Kilvády, Oliver Koch, Cynthia Loemij, Valentina Nelissen, Roberto Oliván de la Iglesia, Sandra Ortega Bejarano, Elizaveta Penkova, Ursula Robb, Taka Shamoto, Igor Shyshko, Clinton Stringer, Julia Sugranyes, Rosalba Torres, Marco Torrice, Jakub Truszkowski, Samantha van Wissen, Sue-Yeon Youn

Music
Steve Reich, *Drumming*

Recording
Drumming, Steve Reich and Musicians (1987)

Version with live music conducted by
Georges-Elie Octors

Musicians for the live version
Ictus & Synergy Vocals

Set and lighting design
Jan Versweyveld

Costumes
Dries Van Noten

Production 1998
Rosas, De Munt / La Monnaie (Brussels), La Bâtie — Festival de Genève

Coproduction
De Munt / La Monnaie (Brussels), Sadler's Wells (London), Les Théâtres de la Ville de Luxembourg

Premiere
07.08.1998 ImpulsTanz Wien

Drumming was performed by the Ballet de l'Opéra de Lyon in 2015, and by the Ballet de l'Opéra de Paris in 2017.

Drumming
Anne Teresa De Keersmaeker / Rosas
Steve Reich / Dries Van Noten / Jan Versweyveld

Publishers
Rosas, Brussels
Mercatorfonds, Brussels

Photography
Herman Sorgeloos
Anne Van Aerschot

Authors
Tessa Hall, Julia Rubies Subiros, Noé Soulier

Interview with Anne Teresa De Keersmaeker
Gilles Amalvi
Conducted for the Festival d'Automne, Paris

Translation of the texts by Gilles Amalvi and Noé Soulier
Emiliano Battista

Editing of the text by Tessa Hall and Julia Rubies Subiros
Emiliano Battista

Proofreading
Lindsey Westbrook

Coordination
Rosas Hans Galle
Mercatorfonds Sara Pallemaerts

Graphic design and color separation
Casier/Fieuws
Typefaces Courier, Helvetica Neue Condensed Black

Printing and binding
Graphius, Ghent
Paper Munken Print White 150 grs 1.5

© 2020 Rosas, Brussels / Mercatorfonds, Brussels

Distributed in Belgium, the Netherlands, and Luxembourg by Mercatorfonds, Brussels
ISBN 978-94-6230-268-6
D/2020/703/19

Distributed outside Belgium, the Netherlands, and Luxembourg by Yale University Press,
New Haven and London
www.yalebooks.com/art — www.yalebooks.co.uk
ISBN 978-0-300-25398-6
Library of Congress Control Number: 2020943378

www.rosas.be
www.mercatorfonds.be

Rosas is supported by the Flemish Community and by the BNP Paribas Foundation.

Photographers and performers